Little Fish

Written by Jill Eggleton
Illustrated by Jennifer Cooper

Little Fish went under the stingray.

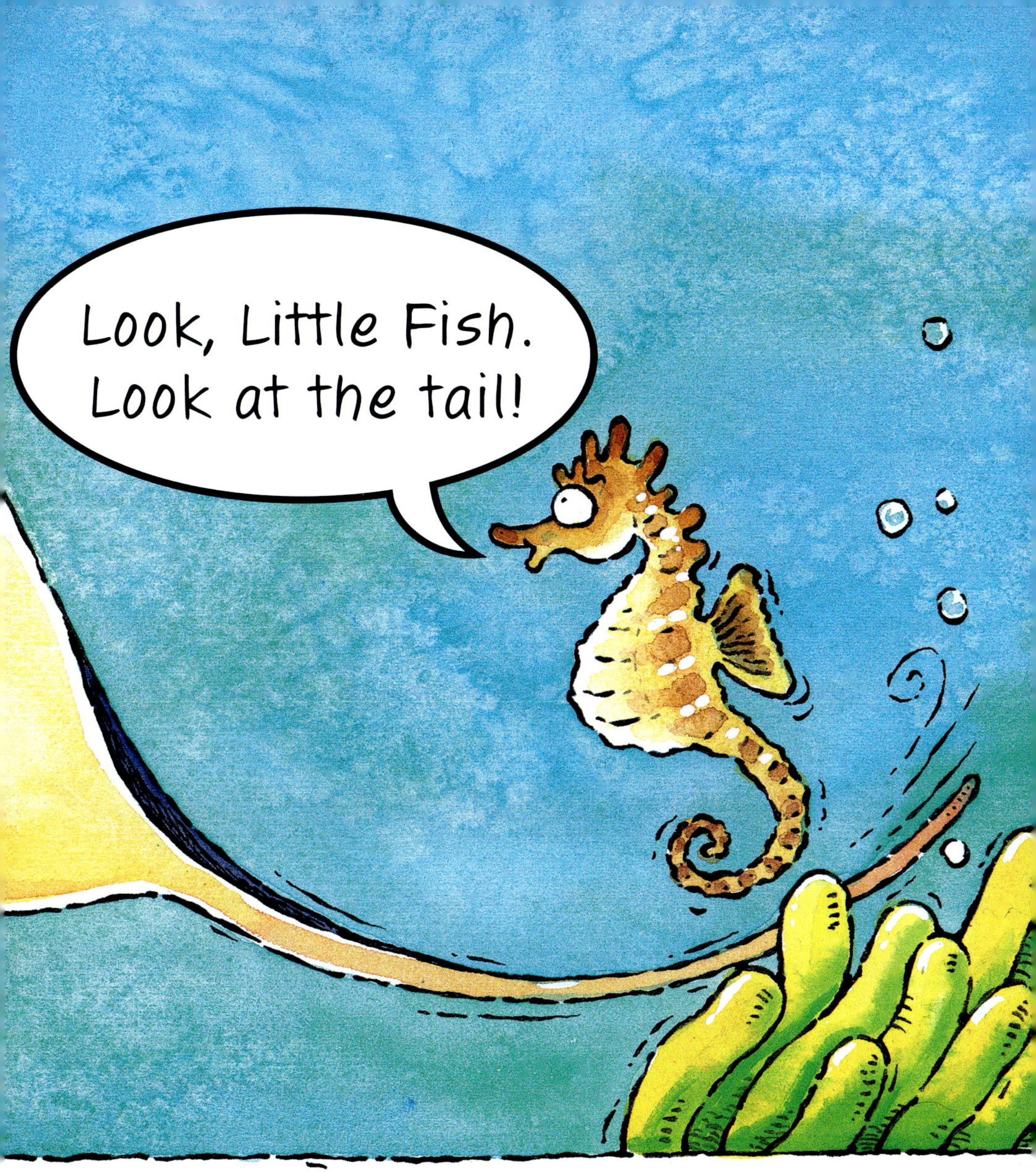
Look, Little Fish.
Look at the tail!

Little Fish went
under the octopus.

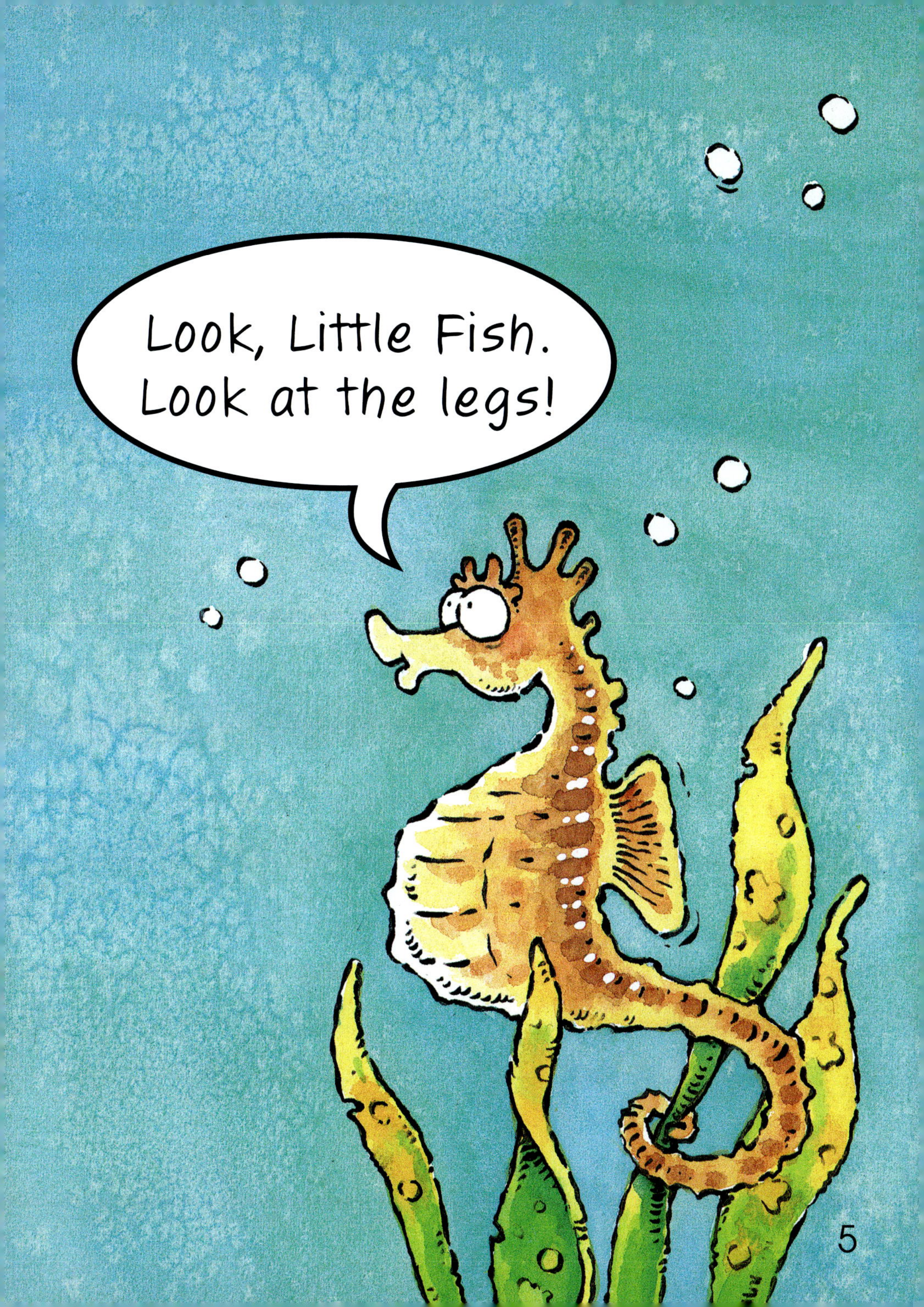
Look, Little Fish.
Look at the legs!

Little Fish went under the shark!

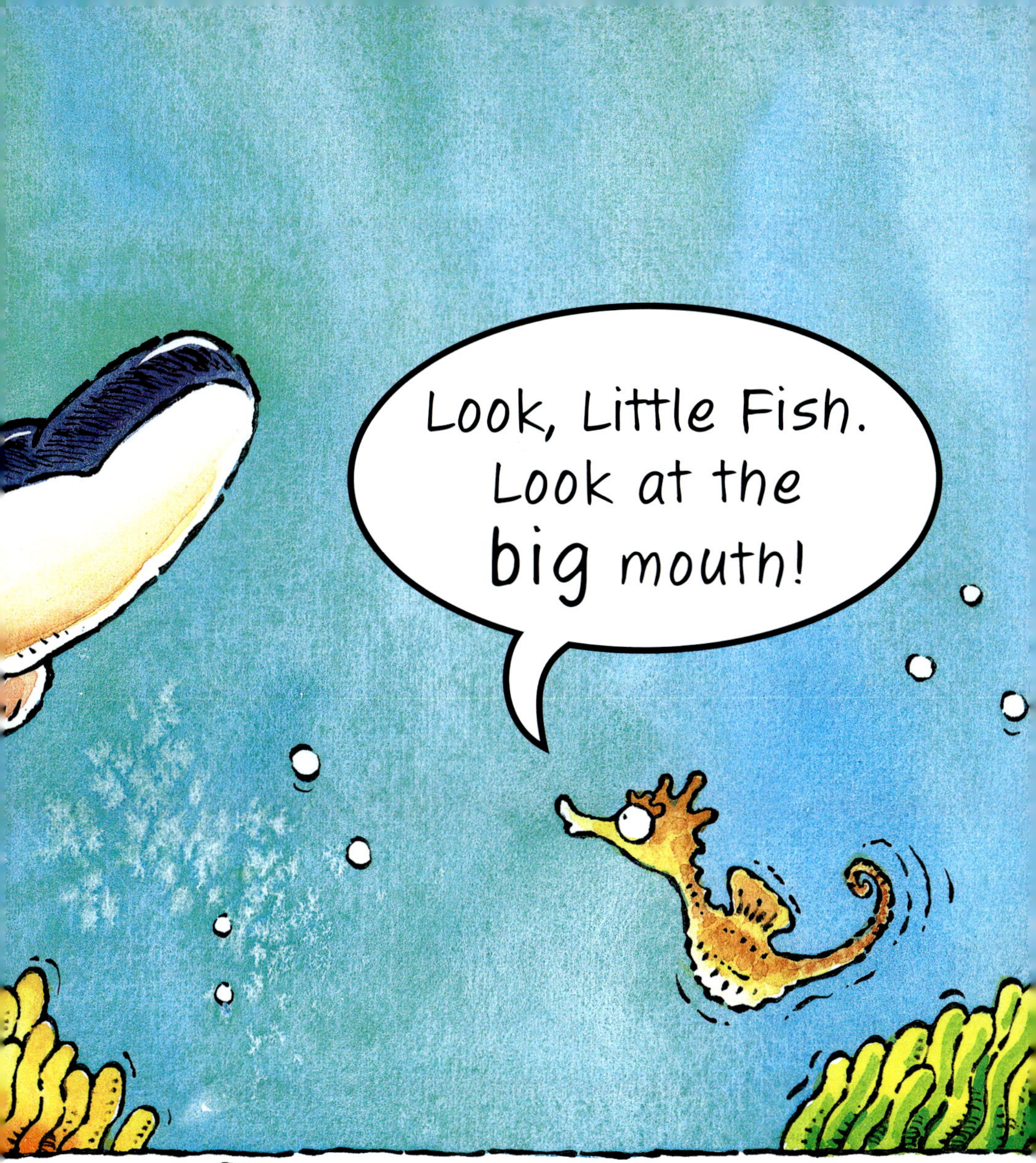
Look, Little Fish. Look at the big mouth!

Little Fish went over the shark.

Little Fish went
into the **big** mouth.

"*Wheeeeeeee,*"
said Little Fish.
"I am in a cave!"

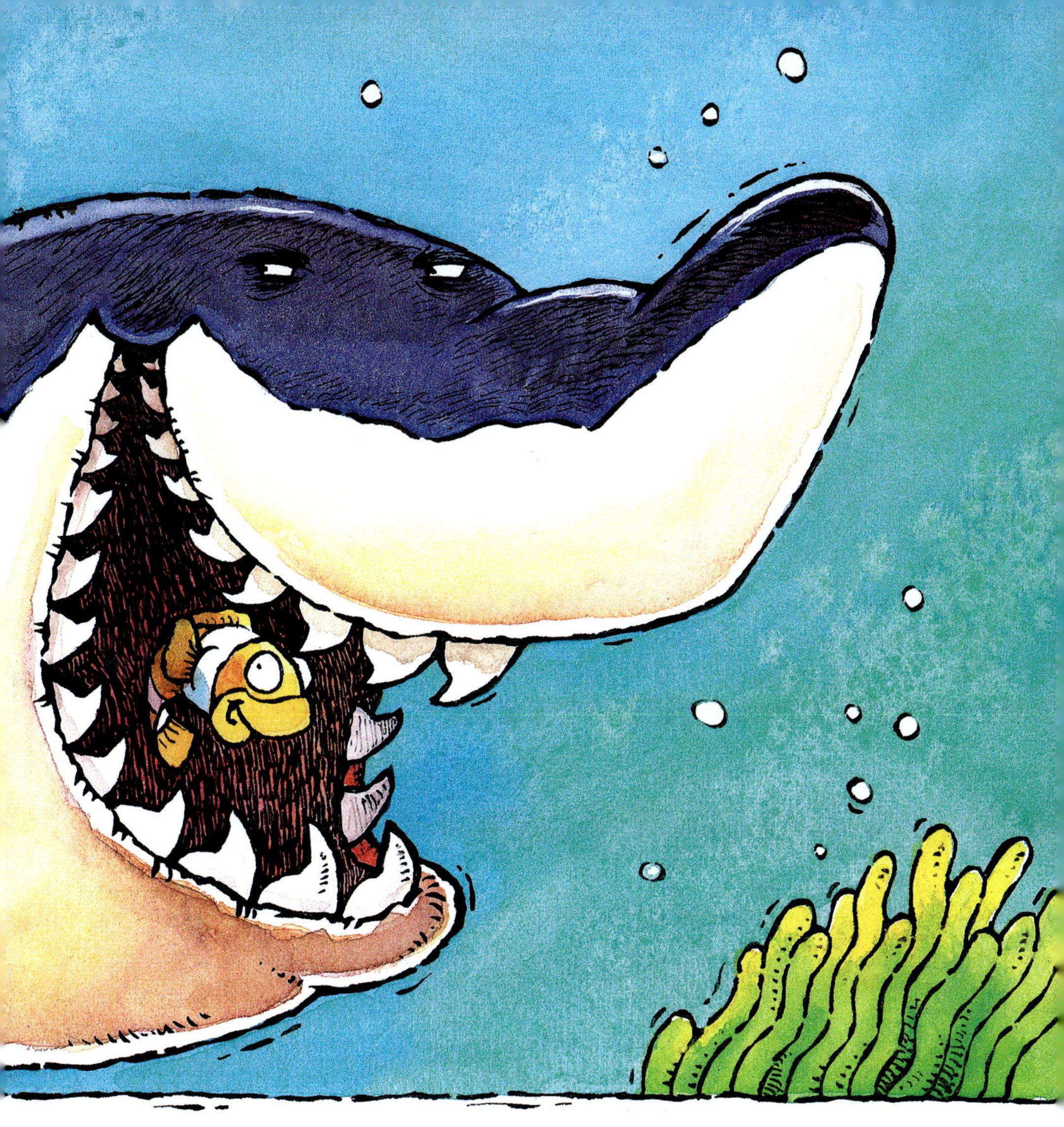

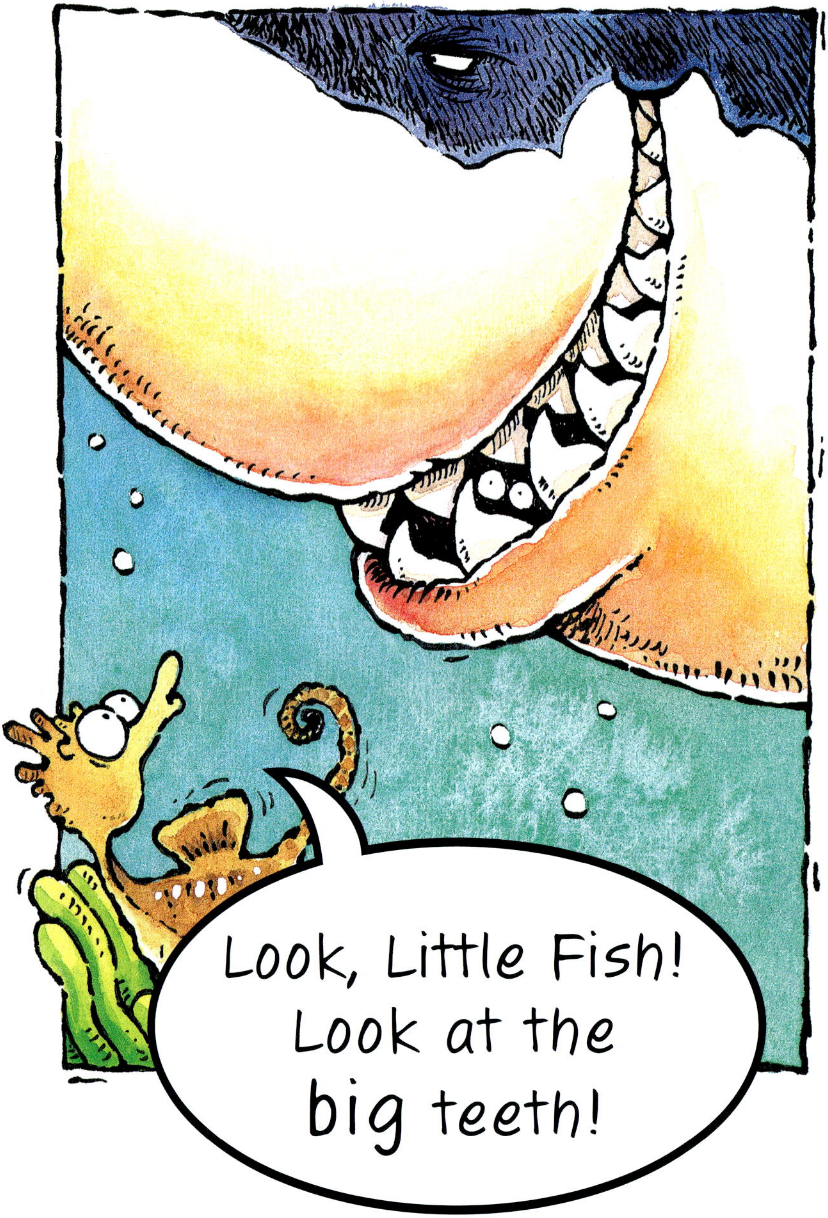
Look, Little Fish! Look at the big teeth!

Little Fish looked at
the big teeth!

"**Eeeeeeeeeek,**"
said Little Fish.
"I am in a shark!"

Speech Bubbles

Here comes a little fish.

Yum! Dinner!

You are in a shark, Little Fish.

I'm going!

Guide Notes

Title: Little Fish
Stage: Early (1) – Red

Genre: Fiction
Approach: Guided Reading
Processes: Thinking Critically, Exploring Language, Processing Information
Written and Visual Focus: Speech Bubbles

THINKING CRITICALLY
(sample questions)
- What do you think this story could be about?
- Look at the title and read it to the children.
- Why do you think the sea horse told Little Fish to look at the tail on the stingray and the legs on the octopus?
- Why do you think Little Fish thought he was in a cave?
- Why do you think the sea horse was trying to protect Little Fish?
- Why do you think Little Fish didn't know about the dangers under the water?

EXPLORING LANGUAGE

Terminology
Title, cover, illustrations, author, illustrator

Vocabulary
Interest words: stingray, octopus, shark
High-frequency words: little, looked, into
Positional words: over, into, under, in

Print Conventions
Capital letter for sentence beginnings and names (**L**ittle **F**ish), full stops, commas, quotation marks, exclamation marks